FREEDOM

OVER

ANXIETY

*4 Simple Steps to Crush Your Fears
and Love the Person You Are!*

A self-help. A how to.
Your journey to wellness. A guide and
champion on your way to becoming anxiety free.
In four simple and easy to use steps.

Christopher Moss

Will You Dare?

Dare you choose hope?

What life could you have with your anxiety as a friend by your side?

Are you willing to find out?

Dedication

A big thanks to my wife and to you. I dedicate this book to everyone of you that is suffering. You are warriors but your time suffering is coming to a close!

Disclaimer

Freedom over Anxiety is meant to guide you on your journey from anxiety to living a life you will love. It is meant to help you develop yourself into the person I know you can be.

This book deals with a lot of hard topics, but it is meant to be inspiring. It is not intended to replace professional help.

This book is designed to be informative and educational. It does not replace medical judgements, therapy or other higher treatments.

I am unable to respond to specific questions or comments about your personal situation, diagnosis, or treatment. I am also unable to give any clinical opinions. If you are in urgent need of assistance, I advise you to contact your local emergency services or local mental health crisis hotlines.

My resources mentioned in this book are used to help and guide you. It is for education and information only. I am not a medical professional. Please do not replace my information for a specialised training and professional judgement of a health care or mental health care professional.

Neither the author or publisher can be held responsible for the use of the information detailed in this book.

Table of Contents

About the Author

Christopher Moss is a best-selling author in three countries. His first book, *Hope over Anxiety*, was downloaded more than 1,600 times. He is married with two children and lives in Northamptonshire, England. Chris has worked in retail for over 28 years and is currently a store manager, author, and life coach.

Chris has a passion for writing, building life skills, and inspiring others to take control of their anxiety. His mission is to give people who are suffering the skills and tools they can use to break free on their own. To create a life that they want. To utilise the skills they have from anxiety. To be the best version of themselves they can be.

Want the first 6 chapters of my first book HOPE OVER ANXIETY *for free?*

Please visit:

https://mailchi.mp/b7273d91423c/landingpage

INTRODUCTION

Your Time To Shine

My Promise To You . . . If you follow this book . . .

You will feel the most alive you have felt in your life. You will feel the calmest you have ever felt. You will have many tools to use to help you with your anxiety. You will be able to use everything you have learnt to leverage your anxiety in order to shine in your life, and you will love the person you are. Your dreams will be ever closer.

Can't be bad, can it?! Want to know how you can do it?

Read on . . .

Hello, and welcome to *Freedom over Anxiety*. Thank you for buying this book. I am excited to show you what can be achieved despite having anxiety. I have gone from crippling anxiety, even struggling to leave the house, to now using my anxiety to be the person I know I can be. And I still have anxiety!

This book IS for you if:

- You need to change.

- You are tired of anxiety, sick to the back teeth of it!

- You are fed up with your life and want real purpose and meaning.

- You want to find ways of loving yourself, of having a big swag bag full of tools to guide you through your struggles and take you on a journey to a life you only dreamed of having.

This book ISN'T for you if:

- You don't want to take responsibility for where you are (not taking the blame; that's different).

- You fancy reading an anxiety book but don't want to take action.

- You just want to feel sorry for yourself; if that's the case, then this isn't the book for you.

If you do want to change and need a quick and actionable book, then read on. I would love to guide you to where you deserve to be!

Your first step to becoming the person you have dreamed of is just beginning. I can't wait to get started with you!

This book is short and sweet. It's a quick pick-up; read it cover to cover in one sitting. It's your companion. It will help you reach your potential. It will help you break free from anxiety using the four steps of progress: calm, understanding, courage over your fear, and happiness.

This book is laid out to inspire you to make a difference in your own life. I have made a promise to you. It's worth repeating: You will feel calmer. You will feel more in control of yourself and your anxiety. You will know what your triggers are and how to tackle them. You will feel empowered. You will have a life back. Don't believe me?

I have clawed myself back from the depths of despair and crippling anxiety. I am proof that with determination and sheer bloody will you can succeed. You can have the life you only dreamed of. I am now coaching others to break free from anxiety. I know this system works.

It worked for me and for many others!

With the steps and skills outlined, you will feel like you can take on the world. More importantly, you can take on anxiety.

I want to let you in on a little secret. I don't *want* to be anxiety-free! 'Why?' I hear you ask. It is simple. I feel that I can now use my anxiety to drive me. Without my anxiety, I wouldn't be me. I would never have felt this way three years ago. I was desperate to remove this pain. Now is a different story. I have gained so much from my anxiety. I would struggle without it. More importantly, I wouldn't be me.

Having anxiety can be a blessing and a curse. I have suffered anxiety—badly at times—for over 32 years, beginning with the death of my brother (my family lost him to cancer when he was just a toddler), and coming to a head three years ago when I was a victim of an armed robbery.

That moment was a gift. Not many people have the opportunity to face death and realise they hadn't been good enough and to make a major change in their life. I will discuss more of this later.

I have struggled. My anxiety has held me back in my life. Now I use it to keep me motivated—to shine, to be a me that I actually like!

I have spent hours upon hours doing internet searches, and I read and listened to books on every possible subject that would help me with this book. I have researched through YouTube, and I have written down my experiences—both the good and the bad.

What an amazing year I have had! My first book became a bestseller. I have had so many people tell me how much it made a difference to them! This is the sole purpose of my writing: to help you. My life coaching has taken off, and I am helping others see what is possible despite the suffering.

This book is what I have achieved. Eighty-one percent of people want to write a book. One percent do so. I was part of that one percent! Then my first book went even further than many first books do, and not just by a small increase. I became not only a bestseller but also an *international bestseller*!

Little old me. It shows what you can achieve if you work hard at it. What can you do? I have achieved something amazing, but I know you can do better!

I also have a life coach. I want to go forward faster, and I need that additional help. It has been brilliant. I have learnt a great deal from him. In this book, I have used some of the techniques he has given me.

We sufferers can utilise our anxiety and creativity to its best outcome.

This book is laid out in a simple manner with no real jargon. The chapters are laid out as the heading suggests, with an inspiring quote about the content and a brief recap at the end called 'in a nutshell.' I have used a few chapters from my first book, but most are new. The book is split into steps, with some breakout action points and food for thought. It can operate alongside my first book, or it can be a stand-alone in its own right.

I use my own experiences to show you how I deal with them. I am as honest and frank as I can be. I have written this book as if I am sitting with you having a cup of coffee. I'm sharing my experiences to help you. Champion you. Believe in you—even when you have stopped believing in yourself. I never had a fellow sufferer by my side during my tough times, so I know what it's like to feel isolated and alone or to feel that no one else feels this way and they don't understand. That's why I want to help you achieve what is possible.

By the end of the book, you will love your anxiety and use it to shine in life, heading towards the person you only dreamed of becoming. How would that feel to you? To no longer feel that your anxiety is a curse, but something that can be amazing? To see anxiety as something you can use, that can be a companion, a friend by your side.

This will happen if you follow this book. Let's get started on your path to being a better you!

I can't wait. Can you?

STEP ONE

Getting to Know Yourself

---

*"You never know how strong you are . . .
until being strong is the only choice you have".
—Cayla Mills*

What is this chapter about?

This is an introduction to me. It is about why I started suffering from anxiety, the lowest point of my life, and the climb back up. It describes how I rebuilt my life piece by piece.

As a lad, I was quiet and shy. My life was pretty typical for a family with three children. I was the eldest. I had a brother Andy he was 7 and Thomas born on the 10th July 1983. We used to play together all the time. I remember the three of us playing with cars made from cardboard and cling-film. I have fond memories of this time.

We discovered that my youngest brother had cancer in his eye. He had it removed. I recall the journeys to St Bartholomew's hospital in London. Mum stayed over to be with him. They thought it was gone. It wasn't. He got this wicked glass eye: I felt it in my hand. It looked so real. It even had veins in it. The detail of the colours was amazing. I had never seen anything like it.

He started getting worse. He didn't want to eat. We regularly went to the doctors but they would just say it was a virus. We didn't realise how serious it was getting. We were advised to give him lucozade to help, but he was still struggling. My brother got progressively worse, so much so he would lay slumped on the settee not really moving. I wanted to help him. I could see this fun-loving boy just laying there. He was not eating or playing—just laying there.

During all of this, I contracted chicken pox. I was the first in my family to get it. This just added even more stress for my parents. Two sick children.

My brother got so bad that we called an ambulance. I remember my father coming back after we put Thomas in the ambulance and looking at my mother and crying. He was so weak he couldn't sit up.

I saw all of this unfolding, and I felt worried and helpless. I couldn't understand what was happening. It was serious. I knew.

He was in intensive care for over a week. He lost more weight. He was completely unrecognisable. March 12, 1985, will stay with me forever. It was the day my life changed. My father came to pick us up from the bus stop after school. I looked at him and knew. 'He has gone, hasn't he?' I don't remember anything else from that time. I just remember going back to school after it happened and feeling that my world had become darker. My world was no longer the same. Neither was I.

My sister was born on 1st March 1985. It should have been such a happy time. But in just 11 short days joy turned to despair.

I blamed myself. I felt that if I hadn't brought chicken pox into the house he would still be alive! This was a mess I created. This was all me. I killed him. I caused all this pain to my mum and dad, to my brother. This was the start of believing I was a victim. That I deserve all the pain and suffering.

When we went to say goodbye to him in the coffin, his yellow blanket that he loved between his legs with his favourite cuddly toy. My mum was stroking his face and saying goodbye to her little boy. He looked greyish. I touched him. He felt cold, like ice. The cold and shock went right up my arm. I couldn't touch him again. I couldn't say goodbye. But he looked at peace. Quiet.

Gone was the little boy who would play with a yellow truck on the stairs. I felt isolated and alone. I felt my childhood died with him. My spark went away.

I felt I had been through hell. I felt I didn't deserve any happiness. I deserved to be bullied. I deserved to be sexually abused. I went through my life expecting to fail and I was prone to self-sabotage when things were going well.

My life up to that point hadn't been great. I had taken a great relationship with my wife and smashed it to pieces. We had money worries. We struggled with the children. I struggled at my job. I felt I had failed and couldn't do it. I was useless at my job. So many mistakes. Shame and vicious mind talk were my most constant friends.

I used my smartphone to escape, to live in another world—in a game, shutting myself off from the people close to me. All my time was spent immersing myself in this world—living another life.

December 12, 2014 5.55am

It was a cold day. It was eerily quiet. As I made my short trip down the road to my work then entered the car park. Something didn't feel right. My intuition was screaming at me. *Go home! Just turn around!*

Who will open the shop? I shot back. *I have to go in!*

I opened the door and went to turn off the alarm. That's when he shot in and grabbed me. I remember shouting out 'Oh, for f**k's sake!' He carried a hammer. The ordeal lasted for 45 minutes. He was getting more and more heated as the experience continued. He wanted the safe open, but he wasn't prepared to wait for the 20-minute safe timer. Every time he demanded it, I put the code in well before 20 minutes passed, it reset. We had one last chance. If we didn't open the safe correctly this time, it would be over 30 minutes. He kept lifting up his hammer threatening to smash my head in.

During the ordeal, I kept telling myself that it was just an irate customer deal with him. Get him out of the shop, then you can deal with all of it. Don't be a d**k. Your children won't be without their father and your wife without her husband. Your actions have to be measured. Be calm.

I was assertive in trying to keep the robber calm, managing his expectations, and trying to ensure that my life wasn't about to be finished so soon.

I looked back on the ordeal afterwards on CCTV. My hands were held as if I was in prayer. I couldn't believe how calm I was. Several times, I felt my life was over. My life was worth £3500. He said he needed the money for his kids. He traded my life for such a pitiful amount of money.

I got the store set up once he had left out the back. The police arrived and advised me to go home, as I was showing signs of shock.

I stared in disbelief: what just happened to me? No, it couldn't have. I was trying to process what had happened. Once that subsided, I started to fall, to plummet. I felt anger. As it coursed through my veins, I tried to suppress it. I felt shame. Like I deserved it. I was alone for long periods of time at home, with too much time to think. Too much time to wallow in my own self-pity.

I would watch TV, anything to keep me from remembering. I lived for the times I couldn't feel anything at all.

My home became my fortress, the place I could feel safe, at least some of the time. The robber knew where I lived so he could come into the house at any time. I would have nightmares about him, dressed all in black, a silhouette at my back door with a hammer in his hands ready to come kill me. That feeling of impending doom and death haunted me for hours after I woke up.

I spiralled lower and lower into despair and panic. My phone became my escape; when I played games I could get lost in them and pretend everything was okay. Except it wasn't. I couldn't leave the house. The effort to put one foot outside the door every morning to take my children to school was massive. I felt I had no choice but to do it for them. Trying to get out of my bed was challenging. I would just lay there motionless with no expression on my face. I even stopped shaving.

I never wanted to leave my bed.

At night, I found it the worst. Bottling up my emotions would cause me to have an outburst out at night. I couldn't look in a mirror. I felt shame. I felt tired and angry all the time—angry at the world for doing this to me, angry at myself because it was my fault, and angry that I had made a mess of yet another job.

My mind-talk constantly pointed out my failures.

I wanted to end my life. I didn't want my family to see me suffering, so I hid my pain. I just wanted to walk off and die somewhere. I thought they would be better off without me in the long run. My wife would be able to move on. I was just this anchor—this emotional burden draining everyone around me. I was sick of all the wars inside my head. I was sick of everything. I didn't want to feel anymore because all I felt was pain and self-pity.

I kept going to see my GP, worried that he would send me back to work. It was an anxiety in itself. I had to escape that place—just too many memories. I had to find another job.

Three months after the armed robbery, somehow, I got another job. How I managed to get through two interviews in a day, I have no idea, but I did it. The pressure I put on myself was immense. I had to go back to work to survive financially.

I have no idea how I got through. I did.

I wasn't fixed. I was a mess. But I put on my best fake smile and pushed forward. I felt I would be sacked anytime. I felt people were going to stitch me up. I was paranoid and worried. I felt that I was a fraud not good enough at my job. All I wanted to do was escape and go to the safety of my home.

I can't specifically pinpoint my lightbulb moment, but something changed in me. I started using my anger and fear towards the robber to spur me on. You won't break me! My stubborn arse. One of my biggest failures was my biggest strength. That will to roll my sleeves up and keep fighting pushed me forward.

I started devouring inspiring self-help books. This was now my driving force. I started seeing the world differently. I realised something. My ordeal was a gift! I had the chance to rebuild myself piece by piece. I had the chance to look at my life, the impact of death, and my own mortality. I faced death. I realised up to that point I was a joke. I was a man who found it easy to play victim to shut off my own pain. I was too worried and selfish. I wanted to distance myself from the man I was. I realised—from reading—that I had really bad. It was even worse than I thought.

I learnt what my triggers were. I learnt who I was. I hated the man I was. I started using the books I read to find what I could do to help myself. I discovered *Jobs* by Walter Isaacson, a brilliant "warts and all" book about the flawed genius who got sacked from his own company but came back and became one of the most innovative men in history. This man built the iPod, iPad, and iPhone, to name just a few. If he can do it, then I can make a difference, too. But what can I do? I want to help people. I want to reach out and show people their best selves!

I set ambitious goals for myself to move forward, challenges that would drive me, now and in the future.

I started listening to inspiring music. I on put YouTube clips about building confidence and other inspiring videos. I no longer wanted to do this as a 'f**k you' to the robber. I wanted to do it for *me,* to be the best me I could be. I wanted to be someone I would actually like.

This Chapter In A Nutshell

- I was 10 when I started my descent into anxiety and feeling like a victim after losing my brother to cancer.

- I was the victim of an armed robbery around three years ago. I plummeted to the lowest point of my life. It was a defining moment, a true gift.

- I vowed to be better. I wanted to distance myself from the man I was. I devoured books—inspiring self-help books. I drank in the information.

- I learnt who I was, what my triggers were, and what I can do better.

- My life has changed since the ordeal. I have become a person I like.

- If I can break free of anxiety, then you can, too. It starts with your will to succeed.

How I Felt after the Armed Robbery . . .

I would lay there,

The warm light of the sun would shine on my face,

But I would just lay there

Feeling nothing. I would hear from somewhere that I needed to get up,

To take the kids to school

No reaction, no feeling,

I felt the world was in slow motion, my eyelids closed more slowly— time moved more slowly.

I would lay there. Appreciating the numbness,

Knowing that it wouldn't be long before the pain would hit me tenfold

I feel empty. Soulless. Hollow.

I didn't want to get up, I couldn't; there was nothing to push me.

Lifeless, numb, my escape.

My Pain

It has now been over 30 years since I lost my brother.

But you never get over losing someone so close.

Your reality changes to a different world. How you survive is how you cope without them.

It's not the loss that is the hardest,

It's how to go on for the rest of your life without them.

That pain is with me all the time. That loss and all the experiences that went with it.

I have spent so long trying to keep people away from me,

Not allowing people to get to close.

It's been easier in my job, as I move around, and build new relationships.

That fear of vulnerability—the pain and worry that they to will go.

The truth is we will all die. In death, it shows you how important life is and what a gift we have.

Appreciating everything that we have. The people, the experiences, and the pain.

Being close to loved ones is the most important part of my journey. Showing them how I feel and think and sharing in their happiness.

This is what makes me feel alive.

FREEDOM OVER ANXIETY

I am privileged to have this constant reminder, and it makes me live to my fullest every day.

Because you never know what is around the corner.

What is Anxiety?

---

*'Nobody realises that some people expend
tremendous energy merely to be normal'*
—Albert Camus

What Is In This Chapter?

I will explain to you the basics of what anxiety is, what
types of anxiety you can have, some causes of anxiety, and
some basic ways of reducing your battles.

FACT: Forty million adults in America have anxiety (8.2
million in the UK). That's 18.1 percent of the population.

What Is Anxiety?

Everyone has anxiety in one form or another during their life. From being anxious about a job interview or exam or medical test. These are normal emotional states.

It is when we struggle to control these worries that it affects our daily lives. For me, and many others, I have encountered anxiety like a downward, ever-more-challenging spiral.

You Can't Escape Anxiety Once It Finds You

I have general anxiety. I find myself being irritable a lot. I find this so frustrating, and it chips away at my confidence. There are times I feel powerless, a prisoner to my emotions. I want to be a more fun-loving, calm, and confident human being.

General anxiety disorder (GAD) is 'characterised by excessive, exaggerated anxiety and worry about everyday life events with no obvious reason for worry'. (WebMDgeneral)

Take a recent example. I was on holiday. My first holiday in a hotter climate for nine years. The place I stayed was amazing. The weather was awesome. We swam in the sea, with the fish. I love to snorkel. Putting bread in the sea, watching thousands of fish feeding was an amazing experience. It was great spending time with my daughter, son and wife without the pressures of work. But one thing was worrying me the entire time. It was the fear of coming back to work and being sacked. It was irrational. It was ridiculous, but it gnawed at me the entire holiday. It was almost like my mind was trying to stop me from enjoying an amazing experience. Like it didn't want me to be happy! So it came up with something tenuous to worry.

I struggle with anything outside my comfort zone or out of my norm. I procrastinate or stick my head in the sand and don't do it. The struggle to actually achieve is a massive battle. This has cost me so much in my life. So many times. Doing the same thing. I can't do it. It's like having to climb a huge mountain. The constant invasive depressing mind-talk.

I recently had an anxiety attack from worrying about a promotion. I had brought my son a keyboard, for my sins. The music was blaring, my son singing away, I was trying to get dinner organised, and my wife was talking to me. The noise in my head and in the house was unbearable. It smacked me in the face, snuck up on me. I couldn't control it.

I had a tightening in my chest and knots in my stomach. I felt like someone had taken the wind out of me. It was my first anxiety attack for months.

People With Anxiety

When I speak to people with anxiety, I am amazed by how many of them I would not expect to have it. On the surface, they seem so normal. They manage to control it and appear like they are not dealing with anything.

Anxiety has three sides: mental, physical, and emotional. Our self-talk is of worry for the future. Emotionally, we feel fearful. Physically, we are tense.

Fascinating fact: More than 70 percent of your body's systems are used during your anxiety disorder! This explains why you always feel exhausted!

The most common symptoms can be:

- Headaches during which the pressure feels like your head about to explode

- Palpitations

- Dizziness

- Weak legs that feel like jelly

- Feeling unattached to the world

- Tension and muscle aches

- Sweating

- Shortness of breath

- Fatigue and tiredness

- Increased heart rate

- Digestive problems

- Irritability

- Mind constantly racing

This can manifest in a variety of other disorders like:

- Phobias

- Panic disorders

- Post-Traumatic Stress Disorder (PTSD)

- Social Anxiety Disorder

- Obsessive Compulsive Disorder

So many people these days suffer from one form or another of anxiety. I used to live being stressed every day. It isn't healthy and burns you out. It also leads to being anxious.

Anxiety is an isolating experience. It's overwhelming. It can damage relationships with family and friends and can threaten people's careers and lives. Many people don't understand how hard and energy-sapping being anxious is.

Anxiety is so complex and individual to that person. There are a lot of different types of anxiety such as:

Social anxiety – '. . . overwhelming anxiety and excessive self-consciousness in everyday social situations . . .' (NHS.GOV)

General anxiety (GAD) – '. . . anxiety disorder characterised by chronic anxiety, exaggerated worry, and tension, even when there is little or nothing to provoke it' (NHS.GOV)

High performing anxiety – 'High achieving and perfection-ist. Driven by details and order in a desperate attempt to calm racing thoughts, worry, and the fear that invade every ounce of the mind and body . . .'(HEADSPACE.COM)

People can appear to look calm, self-assured, and confident on the outside while drowning on the inside.

There is no reasoning or logic that can help: anxiety is purely an emotional state. Most of the time we know what is happening. We understand the logic and battle it, but we feel we have no control over it.

It took me four weeks just to take some rubbish to the local recycling depot. The thought of going made me anxious and fraught with worry. My stomach was in knots. I was scared. It was one of the few times I couldn't explain why and still don't. I have done it loads of times in the past without problems. This time was different. I had to push myself so hard just to get it done, and in the end, I did it. It only took me 14 minutes to do it. Round trip. I had to listen to marvel music to inspire me the whole time. All this for just five bags of rubbish!

I felt stupid and ashamed afterwards. I asked myself, 'Why the hell did it take you that long?' It's only just down the bloody road. You d**k!'

There are days I have struggled to write this book, not due to time constraints or other commitments, but to the nervousness and worry that comes with writing.

Is this book going to bore people? This book has to be a beautiful piece of work! It has to! What happens if it isn't? Am I telling them the wrong information? Is this book a clever concept or total crap? Will people ridicule me for showing what my innermost fears and thoughts are? Will it affect my professional career, my children? These are just some of the questions that go through my head.

Some days, it's been safer not to write. But I want to make a difference to people. The only way I will is by giving everything. And, most of all, by pushing beyond my fears.

What Can Cause Anxiety?

Life events – This could be one major event (like mine), such as a death or car accidents or a series of stressful events in which one experiences many different pressures all at once: relationship problems, work pressures, and financial problems.

Self-talk – Being on constant guard for the worse case scenario to happen. Thinking of all the things that could go wrong will prepare you for when it does.

Biological reasons – It is believed that if someone else in your family is anxious there is an increased chance of you having similar personality traits. Both my parents have anxiety.

Evolutionary reasons – Anxiety is an unpleasant experience. It has also been important for our human evolution. When we feel that we are in danger, our body reacts: our hearts beat faster to help supply our blood to our muscles quickly to get us ready to fight or run away from dangers. We sweat to cool down rapidly for a quick response. Both symptoms are common in anxiety.

Fascinating fact: Eating a banana naturally reduces the effects of anxiety!

Who Gets Anxiety?

Fact: One in ten people suffer from anxiety in some form during their lifetime.

According to NHS.UK, women are twice as likely to have anxiety than men.

The study was carried out by the University of Cambridge and Westminster City Council.

In my humble view, a lot of men aren't so willing to be forthcoming about what they have to deal with. There is feeling, especially amongst my generation, that men should not be so open with their feelings or show failings. From my experience of helping sufferers I have seen many men unable to understand what is happening to them. I have seen it to be 90 percent of women admit they need help and are able to understand what they are suffering from.

CHRISTOPHER MOSS

The truth is that anyone, from famous actors, politicians (some of the most famous of all time), to the random person in the street can experience anxiety. It does not discriminate.

Anyone Can Get Anxiety

So many people have experienced it. I once read that anxiety is like having your own drama queen stuck in your head. This is an excellent and amusing description of what anxiety is like. It's your so-called best friend, who knows everything about your deepest, darkest fears, then uses them to exploit and manipulate you. The voice telling you that you aren't good enough, you're a failure, you are useless, and that no one likes you.

The Anxiety Stigma

So many people have anxiety, but the popular view of what anxiety actually is can be so warped. I don't get why people can say things like 'pull yourself together,' or 'it's not that bad, 'it's all in your head,' and 'don't be such a drama queen.'

What people don't get is that your old part of the brain which senses threats is activated just two seconds before your new part of the brain is aware (this deals with rational thought, etc.). This means that you can't control the anxiety. It's already there before you have a chance to control it!

For me, it's very real. It can be exhausting and soul-destroying. I never asked for this. I never wanted it. I have maximum respect for those who deal with it every day. I am lucky. I know many other people who have worse anxiety than I do.

Ways Of Reducing Anxiety

Here are a few examples:

- Get a routine

- Schedule things

- Exercise

- Be creative (writing a book, drawing, etc)

- Practice mindfulness

Some Of The Basics

Below is a list of the basics that you can focus on to help improve your anxiety. A lot of these are easier said than done!

- Understand yourself

- Learn more about anxiety—having knowledge is the first step.

- Learn to challenge your unhelpful thoughts. Try to see things in a more balanced light. I use meditation for this. Sometimes it is still difficult.

- Improve your problem-solving skills.

- Find new ways to reduce your time spent worrying.

- Learn ways to be more relaxed.

- Learn methods to prevent you from avoiding anything that makes you feel anxious— procrastination, my good friend.

You don't cure anxiety. Being anxious has an important part to play in your life, you need it.

We can learn to find ways to understand your anxiety. Managing anxiety is your best way to deal with it. Fighting it head on or trying to control it is probably the worst thing to do.

When you start making changes, it will be harder, as up to now you have just been coping with it. The long-term benefits, though, are more than worth it. To break the cycle, you need something different.

Each one of us is different. Understanding your own needs and finding the best ways to manage anxiety for you will ultimately make a difference. In this book, I will help with that.

A Few Questions To Consider

- What makes you anxious?

- How do you think?

- What do you say to yourself?

- How do you feel?

- What are the physical symptoms for you?

This Chapter In A Nutshell

- Having anxiety is normal. It's when our worries become uncontrollable that there is a problem.

- Anyone can get anxiety—you can't run away from it.

- Most common symptoms range from fatigue and tiredness to shortness of breath, palpitations, and increased heart rate.

- It can manifest itself into other disorders, like phobias, OCD, panic disorders, and social anxiety disorders.

- What causes anxiety can be life events, biological reasons (family or parents have it), self-talk, and evolutionary reasons.

- A few ways to reduce anxiety—more detail will be covered later in the book, such as being creative, meditation, and physical exercise.

What Are Your Triggers?

What Is This Chapter About?

This chapter has been taken largely from my original book, *Hope over Anxiety*. It is about understanding what your triggers are and what YOU experience. I have written down what I deal with. It is a very frank and open account intended to help you discover your triggers. Understanding anxiety is fundamental to helping you break free.

My Anxiety

I am in a constant battle: an upbeat, positive, joyful, and fun-loving person with a depressed, miserable, pessimistic, and angry side.

I am very demanding and expectant of myself. I am massively critical and find it difficult to accept anything less than perfect. But with others, I show kindness and compassion. I put people on a pedestal. I expect too much from myself.

This arrogance does me no favours at all.

To constantly be at a level I have no chance of reaching, let alone maintaining, drains me!

I have to have control over myself and over my day. I structure my time as rigidly as possible. What do I want to do? What are my objectives? And what needs to be done? I get anxious even when things slightly deviate from what I planned.

I get mighty pissed off when I get overruled and have to follow a different plan, especially when I know I am right. This adds further weight to my anxiety, especially when most of the time the plan goes wrong, causing me to feel even more anxious, continuing the bad cycle.

I think, *What am I doing wrong? Why can't I do the best I can for the day. Why aren't I allowed to do my best?*

I get nervous. I struggle to contain my feelings. I use the seven/eleven technique: breathe in for the count of seven, breath out for the count of eleven. I tell myself that my best is good enough.

There are times when I need to be left alone with my thoughts. I push the ones I love away. I realise that this is wrong and focus again on my breath and tell myself all I need is at this moment. It calms me. I appreciate again what I have.

I also understand now who I am. I am an introvert, and I need to have alone time. I need that to be the best me I can be.

It gets physically and mentally exhausting fighting myself. I have learned a lot more now, to be understanding and kind to myself, to accept my quirks and vulnerability, to embrace my anxiety.

I feel more relaxed about myself. I am coming to terms with the man I am. To know that others experience what I do and think in a similar way is very comforting to me.

I worry about others. I want to make sure everyone is happy. I notice people's emotional state. Many people have emotional tells—things that show how they are feeling, from a shrug of the shoulders to a curving of the mouth. Worries affect me. I may not show it on the outside, but their emotional state links to me. I have to know everyone is okay.

I get a real kick when I see people happy and others progressing in their life. I get waves of joy. I want to inspire others to do better.

My Anxiety Attacks

My physical symptoms – I slur my words and lose words completely. I physically shake, overcome with fear.

I can get quite petty about silly things. It has to be that way because that's my preference. Do what I ask. Everything has to be that way. Don't argue, just do it!

Fast-talking, stuttering, stumbling over words. Or losing a word completely. I am mortified as I stumble further. Then I try to think of the word, and I only feel more anxious and embarrassed—more words fail me. I feel on show. I just want to disappear. I feel stupid. This is when I have to do something that I am not prepared for. If I am having to talk in front of others, or if I feel self-conscious.

Going quiet, zoning out, and rigidly sitting has happened a few times when I was under the most stress. This is me at my worst. I have had this mainly at work. I can't stop these attacks, they just come over me. I feel paralysed. I witness the whole thing, it's scary as hell!

Memory loss and getting things jumbled up. My short-term memory is bad at the best of times, but when I am most stressed and my anxiety kicks in, I lose important conversations. I can't repeat anything that happened, despite listening the whole time, even things that happened only five minutes ago.

My Biggest Anxiety

My biggest anxiety is not feeling I am good enough— a huge fear of failure stops me from succeeding or doing anything. If it's something I am not confident about, I can't face it. I can't deal with it in any way! I have to really push myself, but I won't be able to do it straight away. It will take several attempts and a lot of positive mind-talk before I can attack it. Even then, I am fearful, racked with worry. It could be something insignificant like a phone call, or doing something I have done loads of times in the past. The slightest knock will take me back to the start, and I will have to do it all over again. The irony of this is that fear of failure is what actually motivates me.

I have to make absolutely sure I have done enough. I will use my old, battered, blue notepad, and before I have finished my day, I will review and make sure that over 90 percent of my jobs have been ticked off. If I haven't, I worry I haven't done enough and that I am a failure. This is when my mantra kicks in, and I repeat to myself *your best is good enough*. I will need to repeat this as calmly as I can to myself whilst breathing through my mouth and nose.

If I have got them all done then happy days! I get a wave of relief—I did it today! I am awesome! I feel good about myself.

I hate having pressure piled on top of me. I find it difficult. I already made plans, then to add to them and without enough time to accomplish whatever it is I'm doing makes me very anxious. Not having finished all my jobs reaffirms to me I am a failure and didn't do anything productive with my day.

I don't sleep well when I have a massively important task. I pile further pressure on myself. I tell myself that my best is good enough—that it's okay to feel like this. But when I am tired or exhausted I lose control, and I can't break it down.

These incidences are getting fewer, and the more confident I have become, the more hope I have.

Many times I will say to myself that I will do it tomorrow, having the intention to do it, but never doing it. I will procrastinate and leave it until I have to then force myself with sheer will to get that job done. As always, when I'm anxious, I leave things to the last minute.

There are days when I have finished work for the day. I am so exhausted I can't keep my eyes open— emotionally spent, needing to recharge and be left alone.

Anxiety At Work

It is only recently that I have realised how anxious I was and still am. My mind is constantly racing, everything I need to do and manage is flooding through me, what needs doing and what we need to plan. I don't just think about the present. I am also juggling the next few months. My anxiety at work is a huge driving force; that energy has helped me stand out, but it comes at a cost. I come home physically and mentally exhausted, my mind turned to mush. I have a demanding job, and I am greatly needed at home, but I have nothing left to give when I get there.

Not being prepared, having to speak up to a group or when we get an unexpected visit is when I get anxiety attacks. In the past, I couldn't speak. Now I can say things, although I am not always confident as my mind is racing 3000 miles an hour. My mind-talk is negative, hammering me, making me feel ashamed.

Take a recent presentation. I wasn't given the information until the weekend before, so I had the added pressure of having to prepare for it whilst I was running a store. Already my head wasn't right before I even started planning it. I was completely anxious and fraught with worry.

This led to knots in my stomach on the hour and a half drive to the meeting. I was thinking about how important this was for my career, how important it could be to my family, and what benefits I would get if I came across well.

I seem to often drive up the stakes, make it more difficult to focus and concentrate on the one thing.

I tried breathing more slowly, noticing my shaking hands, the tight stomach, the feeling of no control, blind panic, and tight shoulders, but it only got so far in keeping me in control. Suffice to say, I didn't come across well. I used to be very good at interviews and presentations like this. No longer.

My mind is always way ahead of everyone else, as I am thinking about everything. I used to get frustrated with people who weren't going as quickly as I was. I couldn't get it.

What I expected of myself and the team was unrealistic, but if I could do it, why couldn't others? I can get quite frustrated with not being able to get things done in order to achieve what needs to happen.

I use meditation to slow my rapid mind and focus on the important things, such as understanding the journey; knowing that I am doing good enough relieves me.

I can use my rapid mind to my advantage if we have an important visit from a regional manager or something needs to be sorted. It can be an extremely useful tool to use to drive me forward to get everything done.

Looking After Myself

I need my sleep. I need at least eight hours a night. If I don't get that much, my nerves come to the fore. I need to feel refreshed, ready for the challenges that face me. Without my sleep, my mind-talk is a lot more negative and it drains me.

When I feel exhausted, I try to breathe slowly and use the body-scan meditation. I will say to myself *"this is me when I am tired"*. This is when I am at my worst with my negative self-talk. Everything is over-whelming; everything is wrong. It is then that I distance myself and push people closest to me away. I deliberately do small things to annoy people, so they don't talk to me. I can't cope. I need my headspace. I will do what I need to be alone. This isn't healthy but I have to have it. I am very selfish at this point. I am very tunnel-visioned. My wife always calls me a complete d**k at this point.

I have recently cut back my caffeine intake to just one a day. I plan to cut it back to nothing. My alcohol intake is pretty much zero anyway. I have done this to help me relax and further aid my recovery from anxiety. The caffeine would just make me so hyper.

How Do I Learn What My Triggers Are?

I recommend that you write down all the worries you have on a piece of paper or in a journal. Rate them out of ten. One being a small worry and ten being a full-blown panic attack. This is what is specific and individual to you. I would do it over a period of two weeks. Keep it safe. The list could be like fear of failure or worries about death. Whatever your worries are, write them down. You can, after two weeks, tackle these struggles. I recommend taking this to a medical professional or a life coach.

This Chapter In A Nutshell

- Understand yourself. Know what triggers your anxiety. By doing this you can get a better understanding of what you can do to combat it.

- Take a few minutes to think about your anxiety and how it affects your day. Write it down. This will help you understand your triggers better.

- Look after yourself. Make sure you get enough sleep, cut back on coffee, tea, and alcohol.

- Be kind and understanding to yourself. You are doing your best. Be fair and look after yourself.

STEP TWO

The Power of Calm

'Your calm mind is the ultimate weapon
against your challenges. So relax'.
—Bryant McGill

What Is In This Chapter?

I made a promise to you that you will feel calmer if
you follow this book. This module is all about
building your inner calm. I teach you how to put
sanctuaries into your day to ensure you feel calm and
in control. It is a proactive routine.

Normally you will go through your day trying to avoid
those triggers when one hits you and—boom—you're
back in survival mode, struggling with the tidal wave

of emotions that overwhelms you. With this module, you can cope with whatever the world throws at you.

It is split into simple sections to guide you through. I also would like to add that what I describe in this module will only take 30 minutes of your day. Not a lot or daunting. You can do more if you wish. I feel this is a small price to pay to be in control of your emotions.

It's split into the following topics:

- Structure

- Meditation

- OmHarmonics

- Sixty Seconds to Success

- Music – changing your mood

These are simple-to-use steps. Please do not feel overwhelmed.

Why Do You Need Calm?

This module gives you all the tools you need to be calm. By the end of this chapter, you will have a clear path and skills to use to ensure your day is structured to aid you and have the most productive day possible. You can do this whilst having fun.

Anxiety thrives in chaos. It loves the drama and conflict that follows. It's like a pig in sh*t having the time of its life. It loves it all. Your mind needs to be tamed. This isn't about going to war. You need a far more caring and compassionate part of you. Don't forget this is part of you, even if your inner drama queen does your head in. I will talk more about it in a later break-out chapter.

It's about being in control of your emotions and not allowing them to dictate how you are going to roll. It's about being in control of your thoughts. Being centered and calm is key for your fight against anxiety.

Being calm requires several tools to get the job done. Please understand that you will always have times when anxiety kicks in. If you can keep the majority of your time calm, you will be amazed by what can happen.

What Is Calm?

There are two dictionary descriptions, got from GOOGLE, that I think both are spot on:

1. not showing or feeling nervousness, anger, or other strong emotions.

2. (of the weather) pleasantly free from the wind.

I feel two is kind of poetic.

What Does Calm Feel Like?

I have worked really hard in the last six months to become calmer. I feel I have dropped by almost fifty percent. For me, this means less slurring and losing words, I push people away less often and don't hurt my loved ones as much. No anxiety attacks in over 10 months! If I make a mistake, that is okay. I will note not to do it again and understand it's my way of learning. I'm learning to be kind and compassionate to myself. I am not perfect. I am a flawed human being, just like all of us are. No longer do I hate the man I am.

It's finding inner peace. It's finding resilience. I'm learning not to panic, to use my breath as my anchor, to feel emotions but not be dominated by them, to not be controlled by my fear.

How awesome will it feel to be calm and in control? Empowering, right?

Getting The Structure Right

All of what I will teach you is about being proactive. It's about making sure your day is as structured as possible. It's ensuring you are calm from the moment you wake up. It's imperative that you do not start your day on the wrong foot. If you do, you will be fighting really hard to get back on an even keel. Most of the time when I start my day off in a negative space, I don't get that balance back, and I am in survival mode all day.

The beauty for me now is that I prepare the night before what I imagine will be a stressful day. I go to bed already in the right frame. I do my gratefulness journal—just five minutes of my time. Then I meditate. If things don't quite work out how I want in the morning, such as my son wakes up early, or I don't have time, I tell myself it's okay. I can then use OmHarmonics in my car for 30 minutes.

I also ensure that the times I go to bed are similar, so my mind and human body clock is already primed for bed.

Structure Your Day – What I Do

Before you get out of your pit, I suggest you meditate for a minimum of five minutes. I usually use this one: https://youtu.be/3RxXiFgkxGc. It usually gets me pumped for the day!

When having your breakfast, make it a ritual. Watch your breath, and use the 7/11 technique. Take it slowly. Get your breakfast prepared, and make that tea or coffee. Make it a joy. I would advise getting up a little earlier to appreciate this. In the quiet, free from distractions, notice your peace, calmness, and joy before the chaos descends. You are already going to feel calmer, less stressed, and be fully armed and ready to take on the world!

Anxiety loves chaos. I pack as much as possible into my day to keep my anxiety quiet. My problem is that I do too much. It's important that I rest.

Gone now are my anxiety-fueled days loaded with worry and tunnel vision. I take my anxiety on with calmness. With a sense of curiosity and fun. The important thing is taking everything with a sense of enjoyment and relishing the challenge. Whatever life throws at you, you can handle it.

If things go south and you don't meditate first thing, that's okay. All is not lost! If you need to get the housework done or go for a walk or drive to work, put OmHarmonics on in the car or listen on your headphones as you do your chores. I will discuss this later in this chapter. Be careful, though. It could send you to sleep, so you will probably need to test it prior to doing this live.

Before you get to work or if you need to slip into another role, from Father to manager, for example, do this routine just before you start your next role.

Find time during your day to focus on your breath. This is your anchor. Even a few seconds will help.

Break time is critical. Get out of your environment if you can, and find a place you can be alone. Put on another mediation: https://youtu.be/6AkEAKtL7a8

Before you get home, do Sixty Seconds to Success—I tend to listen to music that's going to get me pumped and give me a second wind.

Why Have It?

Structure and calm are two great tools against anxiety. You gain control of your emotions and thoughts. Then you take charge of your day. Where does anxiety go after that? It doesn't, as you have the control over it. Cool, eh?

It's about being determined to get it done, to achieve it, to make it a habit. You feel in control, so you stop, but then you slip back into the old habits and fears. It doesn't take long. I am motivated now. I know what the consequences are if I don't follow my structure. I fall back to the person I was. I don't want that. I also know what happens if I do follow my structure. The feelings of calm, the kindness and compassion I have not just for others but for myself. The love of others and the peace and understanding are things. I don't want to give that up. Therefore, I make sure I stay focused on doing what helps me stay calm.

There are times when life gets in the way and prevents you from setting your day up!

You need to be fluid and able to change what you're doing. You should always go with the intention to be calm. Allowing one day to slide leads to another day, and before you know it, weeks have passed, and you are back to square one.

Meditation

What Is It?

Meditation is absolutely paramount if you want to be in control of your anxiety. The great thing is it doesn't have to be in the lotus position. It can be done whilst you are walking. It can be done at your desk at work. It can be for five minutes. You can do Omharmonics whilst you're doing the housework. Pretty liberating, huh?

It is about being present in the moment and using your breath to focus your mind to see your thoughts as just chatter. It's about practising being calm.

A study published by the University of Oxford in 2013 has proven meditation to reduce anxiety by as much as 58 percent in a month!

If you want more information on mindfulness, please read my first book on this subject.

Challenging Your Thoughts!

There are times when you need to question your thoughts. This is especially true when your mind is following the same old negative patterns of self-loathing and churning up all the things you have done wrong and that could go wrong. You have a limit to your energy each day. It shouldn't be focused on all the negative stuff and worries. There is so much joy and so many realisations in life. Don't miss out on the fun stuff. Whilst your attention, your most precious commodity, is focused on the bullshit, there is so much about you to love.

I ask this simple question "Is this a productive use of my attention?" Ninety-nine percent of the time it's not. This usually changes my focus.

OmHarmonics

What Is It?

OmHarmonics is a very recent discovery. What it does is put two different frequencies into your brain through music. One in the left ear, the other in the right. The brain then makes a third frequency with rhythmic repeating sounds and the same frequency of your brain when you are at your most calm.

I still remember the first time I used it . . .

I was pissed, frustrated, you name it! I was late for work. Even if I burned rubber, there was no way I was getting to work on time. How embarrassing! I had just made it halfway to work when I had a phone call from my son's school. He had left his lunch box at home! Again?! I was hammering myself. Why did you not check? You usually do! Why didn't you go look in his bag? What responsible store manager gets to work late? How could you? You're a f**king idiot!

Most days now I am not in this place. I am calmer. I'm more centered. This week was a little different. I had just had a whole week of not sleeping properly, so my structure went out the window, as the excitement of releasing my first book had been my biggest focus. I also had a chest infection, so trying to meditate had become difficult, and anchoring my thoughts had become impossible, as I was constantly coughing.

I decided to put it on during my drive to work. On it went, and, within minutes, I naturally slowed my breathing down. I felt I had dropped out at warp speed. My rapid mind had calmed and become still. Silent. Then the fun really did begin. I felt someone had downloaded a bliss app in the back of my head. All my worries dissipated. It was a beautiful feeling. Observing the autumn trees in the yellows, golds, and reds and watching the leaves fall from the trees, I felt I had gone into slow motion. Seeing people walk by in their own worlds was awesome! It was like I was watching my own film with the sound of OmHarmonics playing. I was feeling content and had pockets of joy!

The great thing about OmHarmonics is you can use it with meditation or instead of it. Some people prefer it, as you don't have to mentally work to get into the moment. Instead, you allow the music to wash over you.

If I don't get the chance to meditate, I use this in my car.

I have a couple of tracks here for you to use:

https://youtu.be/_Xb-vGnXNps

https://youtu.be/Zpf6Nz-MVE0

I have learnt that this works best when I am angry and stressed.

How Do You Use It In Your Day

With mindfulness, you need to find a place to meditate. With Omharmonics, you don't. All you need are headphones. You can do it whilst doing the housework or going for a walk. I have found that it works far better if I am annoyed, angry, or frustrated. It is less effective when I am in my calm state.

Sixty Seconds To Success

Another tool I have learnt from my life coach is the following: It is used between locations or when you need to change your role. So, for example, when you are going from store manager to father. I do this just as I am about to get home. If you need longer to ensure the change is successful, take your time.

Ask yourself what you want to be when you get home or to your next destination. I want to be calm, fun, willing to listen to my wife and children's day without being dismissive. I want to be willing to get all the jobs done and ready for the morning. What do you want?

What Barriers Will I Have To Stop Me Doing This?

Not being centred stops me from feeling like I have a choice, as does allowing my thoughts to take over and allowing myself to get frustrated and fed up.

What Will It Feel Like If I Achieve This?

I will feel happy. I would have ensured that my children get time with me when I am in a good mood. I will feel happiness and feel appreciated. The atmosphere will be great and the children will sleep more blissfully.

Doing this whenever you change roles not only reminds you of what you want, but also encourages you to be your best you. Focusing on what it is you want will have a positive impact on the people that are the most important to you.

Before I get to work. I breathe in for a count of five, hold my breath for a count of five, then release it for a count of five. I am getting myself into my calm state and my more logical brain, so I can manage how I feel and understand exactly what I am doing. As I repeat the breathing patterns, I say I want to feel calm, in control, happy, organised, and caring. I imagine what that will feel like, and ponder challenges I may face during my day that could jeopardise that feeling. I also consider what I could do if that arises. That could be listening to music or 7/11 breathing.

For each role change in my day, I use sixty seconds. I have two changes: when I leave to go to work and going from father to store manager then back. Each time I transition, I do this. I would recommend thinking through what you want to be before starting this off. It can be refined if it doesn't quite work. The goal is to help you to be in the role and behave the way you want. I have noted a remarkable difference in how I approach my family and job since I have been using it. In only 60 seconds the results are pretty cool!

Listening To Music

I use this to manage my moods. I love music, and I can get lost in a song if it moves me. From the heaviest of metal to classical, I find music I enjoy. What music fills you with joy? What do you love to listen to? Write down the answers. Have a collection of music, so you have a variety to choose from.

What songs make you feel happy? Fill you with joy?

What songs pump you up? Make you want to dance? Sing out loud?

What songs calm you? Are slow and moving?

What songs inspire you?

Have these written down and then use them to take you out of a bad mood or whenever you want to be inspired. Music helps to rewire your brain to be more positive, but it's an awesome tool for your swag bag to control how you are feeling. It's a mood changer. How powerful does it feel to know that you can change your day by listening to music?

Choosing What You Care About

Worries affect all of us. Our mind is constantly finding struggles and stress to think about. It's there to find the threats. We can decide whether it's worrying about having one hair out of place (not recommended) or the bigger things like funerals or worrying about big decisions. The old comment, "There is only so much love to go round" applies here. This time to care. If you want to put all your anger or frustration into something that means sh*t, go ahead. But in truth that doesn't really matter. Care about the big stuff.

News Flash!

Problems don't go away. They change. They become better problems. But you never really have none. The way I look at it is as this. We all face challenges. The only way you can grow and experience the amazing highs of life is to experience the lows.

Talking of problems, I can compare myself to where I was at three years ago. Straight after the armed robbery. I felt the lowest I have ever felt. I lived for the times when I felt nothing at all. I felt useless, a failure. I was worried about money. What were we going to do after Christmas with no money? How much did I need to escape the job? To escape me!?

Now my concerns are different. How can I enjoy my life more? What do I need to do to drive my books? To make more money? How am I going to launch my coaching? How is that going to work for people? How am I going to move my team and job forward? Massive change, isn't it? Don't compare, do they?

Sleep

Anxiety loves to keep you awake in order to control you. Lack of sleep is a major problem for us sufferers.

Go to sleep at the same time every night—make it a routine

Wake up at the same time each morning and set an alarm if you need to.

Sleep in a cool room.

Ensure the room is dark.

If you need it and can do it, take a nap. I call them power naps. Make sure it's under 40 minutes, or else you won't feel the benefits.

Thriving Forward

Being calm can do some amazing things for you. It can keep you in control of yourself. It will help you remain in the human part of the brain more often than not, and its presence means that you will be more capable of moving forward in your life. You can be your best you, and ensure that you continue to achieve what you want to achieve in your life.

Now that you are at the end of the module, I know you now have the tools to be calmer. To lower your anxiety dramatically and enjoy life more. All of this works if you use your tools. If you want to stay calm you have to follow the structure every day.

This Chapter In A Nutshell

- Being calm is your ultimate weapon against anxiety.

- There are five ways that I recommend helping you be calm; structure, meditation, Om-Harmonics, Sixty Seconds to Success, and listening to music.

- You have a limited amount of energy and care. Choose what you care about wisely.

- You will always have struggles. It's how you see them and approach them that will be the difference.

- Being calm using a structure is the corner-stone of everything else. Keep to it, and you will find you have more control and can manage your anxiety better.

Tools For Your
Swag Bag . . .

You're p*ssed off, annoyed at someone. You're mad and frustrated.

You are also annoyed at yourself that you handled it shockingly. You lost it. Control over myself is so important to me. I need to feel I am managing every situation correctly in a calm and kind way.

I will write down how I am feeling. It helps to get it all out!

Journal your feelings, and be open and honest. You can also use your left hand if you are right-handed. This will make you more frustrated and angry.

Split it up into three parts.

1. **Be as petty and immature as you want. Get it all out of your system.**

2. **Then write down how the other person might have been feeling.**

3. **Now write down how you can handle the situation and your feelings in a way that produces your desired outcome.**

This is about priming your mind for next time and ensuring you can stay in control of your behaviour when a situation arises in the future.

Writing it down helps to release your frustrations. Get out your anger and hurt. Then come up with a plan to ensure you are in a stronger frame of mind next time.

I have used this tool a lot since my life coach taught it to me. I find it can clear my mind and ensure a better outcome the next time I'm triggered by intense emotions and anxiety. Reframing my view, seeing things more clearly and from an enlightened standpoint has helped me make tremendous progress in my life.

It's great to just write all your crap and anger down on a piece of paper. My handwriting is awful, so I know most people will have no clue what I have just written. Just getting it out allows me to find relief.

Give it a go. Next time someone pisses you off, say to yourself, "I am going to write this down." Even during the situation, know that you can have a release from this anger and frustration.

Some people aren't going to behave the same way you do and are going to do things that annoy the hell out of you. That's life. But you can choose how to respond to it. Using tools that work will ensure a better outcome next time.

A few more tools for your swag bag!

I listed a few in my previous book *Hope over Anxiety*. I wanted to add a few more here. With this you can use the ones that you would like to do the most. If one doesn't work for you. That's fine. You can choose another. They are here so that you can bring out some more tools when you need them. To give you a feeling of empowerment. *Its okay if I have worry and panic because I know how to get out of it.* Most of these tools I found on Bustle.com. DR Sarah Allen has some excellent ones here. I picked and have used the best ones. There are many more on the site.

It's here to give you a sense of confidence and control.

Tools for your swag bag 1 – Using an elastic band.

Put a elastic band on your wrist. Have it on all day. When you start to panic, worry or feel low. Ping it. Use this as a distraction technique. It will stop your negative thoughts even for a short period.

Tools for your swag bag 2 – Plan time during your day to worry and be anxious.

Say what? You actually want me to worry? Haven't you been teaching us the exact opposite of this? Challenging your thoughts. Letting your thoughts go? Yes, but there is a little twist to this.

Plan it into your day. If you need five minutes cool, ten, thirty or one hour. It doesn't matter. What is important is that you hear what you are struggling with. Suppressing your anxiety and feelings is the worst thing you can do.

It is important to allow your feelings and worries to be heard. Meditate beforehand. Allow your worries and anxious thoughts to come to the surface. Write them down. Then find ways to resolve those worries. To find solutions.

This is an excellent tool. It means you are listening to your feelings, allowing your feelings to come to the surface and able to manage them. On your terms! By listening and resolving your worries it will give you more control over what is happening. It has been proven to quieten your worries. You are also rewiring your brain to think differently. You can also say to yourself, I will deal with that during my worry time. Quieten your worries further. (Bustle.com)

Tools for your swag bag 3 – Box breathing.

I use this for my Sixty Seconds to Success. Breathe in for a count of five, hold your breath for a count of five and release for a count of five. It's about helping you to feel calmer. Say to yourself *'this is me when I worry'*. Removing the emotion from it and allowing your mind to move over to the logical side of your brain.

Tools for your swag bag 4 – When you have a panic attack, do a handstand!

Really?! Yup, really. I have a good friend of mine that does this. She swears by it. Bringing a sense of fun when she is about to have a panic attack. Distracts the mind and you can hardly be serious when you are upside down!

Tools for your swag bag 5 – Have a hot drink or hold ice in your hand.

Another great focus/distraction technique. By holding ice in your hand, you can focus on the cold. How it feels in your hands. The discomfort is an excellent distraction and will give you the power back.

Having a hot drink is similar, but also you can utilise this to meditate in stealth mode. I have described this in my previous book *Hope over Anxiety*. Allow the change in temperature for your body to distract you. Slow down the drinking process. Make sure it's something you love to drink. Smell the scent of the drink. Bring it slowly to your lips. Breath deeply. Let the drink glide down your throat.

This is about intentionally slowing down your rapid mind. Putting yourself into a more calm and relaxed state.

MY INNER DRAMA QUEEN

Rewiring Your Anxious Brain

'You don't have to be positive all the time.
It's perfectly okay to feel sad, angry, annoyed,
frustrated, scared or anxious. Having feelings doesn't
make you a negative person. It makes you human'.
—Lori Deschene

This is understanding your anxiety and rewiring your negative mind to a positive and calm one. You can change how you think! It takes time, willpower, and strength, but it is achievable. I have done it. You can, too.

We have discussed what my triggers are in a previous chapter. This is an amusing tale of what my mind says. More specifically, this is a story about how my inner drama queen behaves. I have done this to show you what tricks they can play. This isn't you. This is your anxiety. It manipulates, bullies, shouts, intimidates, lies, deceives, you name it! It will do everything to keep you in the safety of your box and do anything to have total control over you!

By seeing your anxiety as something separate, you are able to detach yourself from it. It will help you understand yourself better and what can be done to break free from anxiety altogether.

What Does My Two-Year-Old Look Like?

For some reason, I picture him as Sully from *Monsters Inc*, but with a higher-pitch voice. He is selfish, extremely immature, and prone to panic at the first sign of anything happening. He will over dramatise an event or something that happened. He manipulates the truth. He has been prone to shout and bully me into submission. He has also been known to stamp his feet and sulk.

Staying Calm

We have already discussed this in a previous chapter. One of the steps of taking control and thriving as a sufferer is ensuring you have a process for keeping calm. It needs to be more than one thing. There are days when life gets in the way and you will have to have other tools in that swag bag of yours to take out and use. Being calm ensures you stay in control. Being calm ensures you can see anxiety for what it is. Being calm should become your default setting.

Challenging Your Thoughts

I find challenging my thoughts exhausting, but it has been worth the investment of my attention. Even now, my brain is constantly in chatter mode, as I call it, finding a new angle from which I can berate myself for what I have done or not done. It's really important, at least for me, to feel that we all make mistakes. Even with the knowledge and best intentions we are going to get things wrong. That's fine. If you have a chance to make amends, then do so, but what you need to do is be compassionate to yourself when you are struggling and your mind is just hammering you. Note what is happening, and say 'this is me tired', or 'this is me when I have made a mistake'. Bringing your mind into the more rational side will remove the bashing. Other times, asking 'is this a productive use of my attention?' Ninety-nine percent of the time it isn't. Just being aware of what's going on is half the battle!

I also struggle with imposter syndrome and not ever feeling good enough. This manifests itself in me, pushing myself harder to prove I am enough to show I am not an imposter. It's important to understand, and I am getting there, that we all feel insecure about ourselves. All of us have talents and are amazing, but flawed, individuals. I was extremely insecure about myself. That has helped drive me.

What we don't see is that others have internal dialogue; we only see what's on the outer surface. We shouldn't ever worry about or compare ourselves to others. Everyone has their own struggles.

Keep challenging your thoughts. You will find that you will consciously change how you think. Quieten your mind-talk and become less tired!

What a difference it has made for me.

I sleep a lot better now. I am able to get out of moods and anxiety far quicker. I am more resilient. And I see things in a far more positive light.

Avoidance

We anxiety sufferers struggle when there is something that needs to be sorted, especially when it's important. We allow our inner drama queen, our anxiety monster, to grow, so it becomes a huge wall to break down. It can seem nearly impossible. Why do we do that and allow fear to take hold? Why do we think up all the worst-case scenarios and make it as tough as we can??

If there is something massive that needs to be completed or sorted then do it straight away. I would advise you to do it first thing in the morning when your willpower is at its strongest. The feeling you get afterwards when you tackle the problem or job is empowering and gives you a boost. It puts me on an emotional high, preventing my inner monster from growing from a little whisper to having a total hold over me.

Try it. I guarantee that job you have been putting off, that problem that has been gnawing away at you, isn't as bad as you feared and always feels smaller once you have done it. Why put it off?

Your Challenge

Simple, but oh so scary. Tackle that tough problem you have been putting off!

Write down how you felt after you did it:

Guarantee

You will feel 10 times better once you have completed it.

This Chapter In A Nutshell

- In your calm state, you can consciously rewire your brain.

- What does your inner drama queen look like? How does it behave?

- It challenges your thoughts. Every time your mind starts hammering you, ask yourself this question from a place of calm. Is this true? Allow your logical side to kick in and take you away from your emotions.

- Avoid avoiding! Make sure that you tackle difficult jobs as early in the day as possible. Make sure that the big problem you have to deal with is dealt with when your anxiety is just a small voice.

When Life Thows a Spanner into Your Structured Day

One morning, I received a phone call from work, because, due to the weather, we were struggling to open the store on time. The roads were bad. It was my day off. Normally, I meditate and write before I get up to set me up for the day. When I got the call, I shot out of bed, reorganized childcare, chucked some clothes on, and off to work I went.

My panic, coupled with tiredness, took over. I had about twenty minutes in which all I could focus on was getting to work and opening the store. I was worried.

I focused on my breathing and noted my physical symptoms.

The amazing part now is that I can be aware far quicker and also be fluid with what I can do. Now I have tools that help me change my mood and calm down. This has taken practice and, above all else, habit.

We all know that when things happen we have to react. But once your mind is primed, you don't forget to meditate, you look to find ways to meditate, even when things have taken over, even when you're in an anxious place.

I put on some music for ten minutes that I loved. Then I put on OmHarmonics. By the time I had dropped into a calm place, I received a call to say the store was open, so I could turn back around and go home.

When life throws you sh*t, you have to be fluid and find other ways, but find ways you must!

Take Responsibility For Where You Are

'If you take responsibility for yourself, you will develop a hunger to accomplish your dreams'.
—Les Brown

What This Chapter Is About

Your first steps to move forward with your life are in here. If life has dealt you a bad hand, it's important to accept the position you are in. It's not about blame. It's about saying: 'This is me; this is where I am. This is how I feel. Don't blame others'.

We who suffer from anxiety do tend to blame others and find reasons for what we are feeling. We don't want to accept the pain. We don't own where we are.

Self-belief Is Overrated; Take Courage In Just Doing It

What builds confidence or certainty is *doing* and then reflecting on it. I really struggle to talk in front of a lot of people. I physically shake. I slur my words. I have an anxiety attack. I have to really focus on my breathing to slow myself down. My mind is finding ways to escape the situation. I worry about all the worse possibilities. I know each time I face it, I will get better. More confident. I hope that in the future I might even be comfortable doing it. That's a challenge in itself!

Gratitude: you have to feel these positive emotions; it won't work without doing so.

Rewire how you think. Remove the negative mindset.

Move forward with your life.

What You Have Been Through Is Not Your Fault, But Only You Can Change!

My story has been detailed in this book and in my previous book. I could have felt the world is to blame for my anxiety, felt sorry for myself, and wallowed in self-pity. For a long time, I did. When I looked at how I felt, something amazing happened. I moved forward. I accepted my pain and my faults as a human being and accepted what had happened up to that point. There was no blame on anyone, not even myself. Allowing my negative mind-talk to take control would not have helped. This involved taking a long-term view of my life and where I needed to go.

By taking responsibility for where you are, you can grow as a person and heal yourself.

By taking responsibility, you can have the life you want.

What Does That Mean To You?

Accepting my position and tackling one problem at a time was a very positive experience. Take in one problem at a time. Look for the long haul. You won't be done all at once. This leads to far too much pain and frustration. There are no easy options. The benefits will last a lifetime!

How Do I Do That?

Go deep into yourself. If you need to write down what hurts, what bothers you. If you don't do it, that's cool as well. What is important is recognising where you are, what you are feeling, what experiences you have had, and what needs to come next are up to you. It is about understanding where you are emotionally. It's taking that emotion from the place you are in and doing something about it. Be very honest about it. This is a conversation with yourself. No judgements! Be as honest as you can.

If you need to seek help, then do so. It's about doing something about it; fixing yourself.

There is so much information available to you on the internet. There are several Facebook sites, and if you need to talk to others you can. If you don't want to, then friends and family can also help. It's really up to you to decide what your preferences are.

Incidentally, I have a Facebook group that helps others with their anxiety. I invite you to join if you wish.

Please visit the following link . . .
www.facebook.com/groups/1801426393261647/?ref=bo
okmarks

Call To Action

This is one of the most important action points in this book. It will change your life, if you allow it to do so. It's time to stop blaming others. It's time to stop blaming yourself. It's time to change your mentality, change your brain, and how your anxiety thinks. This is the start to rewiring your anxiety.

This shifts your perspective about what you can feel and control. So much of our time is feeling powerless and trying to control what little we can. We feel unable to manage ourselves, unable to deal with everything that life throws at us. But what would happen if you could regain control and strength? Would that be something worth doing? Think about it. By taking responsibility for your feelings, you empower yourself to make changes. I own this. I CAN do something about it!

Know that you have that power over your life, and you can shift your perspective. Once you realise what you can do, just watch what you can do. We are all gods. We make our own worlds. What world do you want for your life?

This Chapter In A Nutshell

- Taking responsibility for your feelings is a game changer in your battle with anxiety.

- Don't wait for when the time is right and you have more confidence. Do it now, and build your confidence that way.

- This isn't about blaming yourself; this isn't about fault. This is understanding that you aren't powerless. How amazing does that feel? You can change YOU. YOU HAVE THAT POWER!

- It's a positive experience and something to be excited about.

- To find out how you are feeling, you need to go deep into yourself.

- One of the most important parts of this book is to take time to see and look at what a powerful impact change can have: it can show you that you create your own world and life.

My Deal with Death

Death: It's time, time to finish this. Time to say goodbye.

Me: No!

Death: Why? You want this! You want to die. I am calling you home.

Me: Not anymore.

Death: I have seen your pain. You have faced your own death. You know it's time to find peace. You deserve to be free from it all!

Me: I am not ready to go anymore! I have seen what I can do!

Death: You are tired of your own suffering in your life, wallowing in your own self-pity, fed up with feeling like a victim. Come on, end this. Find your way home. I am trying to help you!

Me: No. I want to do better. Give me that chance. I can do more. I can be better. Let me live. Let me show that my life can have meaning. Let me help others. I want this more than anything, and I will prove it every day for the rest of my life! Let me show people what they can do with their lives. Please, I beg you, give me a second chance!

STEP THREE

Leveraging Your Anxiety

'I want more, I can do more, I will break this cycle and be the me I have always wanted to be'!
—Christopher Moss

What's In This Chapter?

In order for you to break free from anxiety, you need to know why you can't dream of a better life whilst you are stuck in survival mode. We will discuss what you need to do to be able to get out of survival mode. I will talk you through how you, too, can focus on you and work towards being a better you. I will help you see what is possible and dare to dream of more.

Survival Mode

This is the sufferer's default setting if you like. This is where we are most days. Getting up in the morning and having no sleep, dreading the day ahead, worried about your future and feeling like you have no life and no friends. You struggle to get out of bed and to pretend that all is okay.

How Can You Thrive In Survival?

The truth is you can't. Once your basic needs are met you can then look out to the future.

What Can Your Future Hold?

What people don't see is that they create the world around them through what YOU think and what YOU feel. Challenging your thoughts by being in a calm state can drive you in a new direction.

Focus on what will help you. Tailor your day to help you. If you drink too much caffeine and that affects you, cut back or stop. If you don't sleep, why not? What can you do differently?

Survival mode is your battle setting. You won't get out of anxiety sitting in it. You have to look after you and find ways to ensure you no longer have to battle through your days, so you can look to the future. You start with your calm place.

Invest In Yourself

If that means taking time to read or take a course that will improve you, do it. Look to get a life coach, if you want. You will see dramatic improvements in you. We are not talking massive changes to your journey, but a mere four percent, a small percentage for a dramatic change!

You are in a default setting. Your life will pan out in a basic way by harnessing what you love, what you enjoy, and finding someone who will open the dreams inside of you. That's when your life can really change. Take an adventure beyond anything you thought possible. The beauty of it all is that it's in YOU now. All you need is to unlock it.

Dare To Dream

Anyone can become successful. This isn't about fame or fortune or making a fast buck. This is seeing that you can do things beyond your dreams. What would that feel like?

Survival Mode: How You Feel

- In a constant battle

- Stressed

- Irritable

- Sad

- Depressed

- Exhausted

- Want to be left alone

- Can't function

- Feel lonely

- Can't control your emotions

- Powerless

- Frustrated

- Deeply unhappy

Thriving Mode: How Does That Feel?

- Calm

- Able to think logically

- Happier

- Able to enjoy life

- Want to improve yourself

- Want to help others

- Fun loving

How Do You Get From Survival To Thriving?

Ensure that you have all the basic needs covered and that you feel safe—these include:

- Breathing

- Food

- Water

- Sleep

- Clothing

- Sexual instinct

- Shelter

If you struggle financially or haven't had job security, your mind is always going to struggle in survival mode. We sufferers of anxiety struggle with sleep, which is a basic human need, and as a result, most of the time we will be in survival mode. We will always be fighting, never able to look higher, and want to progress ourselves.

Use the structure I have laid out for you in this book. You will then be able to up your ability to manage your anxiety, feel safer, and build your self-confidence.

What Happens When You Are In Thriving Mode?

Ever seen people that look like they have it together? Who are driven towards their dreams and feel comfortable in their own skin? That would be you. You are able to see when your anxiety is taking hold and to use the tools listed in this book to help you manage it. You are able to reach for the life that you dreamed of, to ask yourself not if I can't reach my ambitious goals but are they ambitious enough?

What are your goals? To be the person you always dreamed of? To use your pain to develop further? To know that this is an amazing adventure? To be creative and think outside of the box?!

To go deep into yourself and know that would be okay.

To want to be the best version of you possible.

To see you can do anything you want. The only limit is what you put on yourself.

Shine your light on the world. Be the best you!

How Do You Really Thrive?

I think some of it can be done by following your ambitious goals. Using YouTube to inspire you will help. Reading also will help. But to really get deep, to push yourself, I would recommend getting yourself a good life coach to have that accountability and to see dramatic major jumps in your life. I feel the only way this is possible is by working with a life coach. Not only will they help you develop now, but you can also use everything you have learned in the future, too. I have one. I intend to always have one. My biggest leaps have been due to the fact I have a life coach. They are there to help you, to serve you. When you don't believe in you, they still do.

Why A Life Coach? Aren't They Expensive?

Life coaches deal in dreams. They unlock dreams you have never spoken to another person about. When I'm with my life coach, I ask questions you haven't ever considered. The effects on your life from a great coach can be life-changing. How much would you put on your dreams? How much would you put on changing your life? To see the world completely differently? How much is that worth? Your dreams should be priceless.

What Can The Future Hold For You?

That's down to you. Do you have a real need to change? If you are, you will. You know what can be achieved in your life, a life beyond what you ever dreamed.

You have it in you now. You know that you are in survival mode. You know what is needed to move forward, to make you feel safe. And you know what you need to go to the next level and to be able to be the best version of yourself, to be that person that you only dream about. In your better days, you get a glimpse of that person and think, *That's me!* You can see that person you can be proud of.

Wouldn't that be something worth striving for?

What Is Your Purpose?

I consider it a basic need to have a goal, to have a dream. Your purpose is the rule that will drive you. Know you have a journey to take, and understand there will be ups and downs, that there will be times of struggle. To be challenged and struggle more than you have ever been, but that's okay because you have a purpose! What is yours? What dream do you want for you? What is your purpose?

This Chapter In A Nutshell

- We, sufferers, are stuck in survival mode and unable to get out and develop ourselves.

- There are basic needs that you need to feel. Without these basic needs, like sleeping well, food, and shelter, you will struggle to thrive.

- Going from surviving to thriving requires understanding what is holding you back and putting skills in place to help you.

- Your future will be far brighter now that you understand what is holding you back.

- You can do anything you want with your life.

Leveraging Your Anxiety

---

*'Without anxiety and illness, I should
have been like a ship without a rudder'.*
—Edvard Munch (Famous painter of The Scream)

What Is The Chapter Is About?

You are now calmer, and you have plenty of tools to aid
you in your day. Loving your anxiety and then using it to
help you will lead you to shine in your life. My biggest
weakness, I always felt, was my stubborn arse. There have
been times that this iron will has been the single reason I
get up in the morning or keep going forward or launching
this book. Where does my drive come from? My anxiety
and my 30 years of pain and suffering have given me skills
that I would badly miss if I no longer had anxiety.

Your greatest strength can be your greatest weakness. There are times when you will feel anxious and have to struggle. I feel that is a small price to pay for the rewards of anxiety. There are several. I am sure you are looking at me sceptically.

Understand Your Triggers

It's important that you understand what your trigger points are, so that you are aware of an impending attack and you can be proactive.

Befriend Your Anxiety

Take a kind compassionate view of your anxiety. Love it. Be gentle. Don't let it rule you. Be assertive when you need to, but be compassionate and kind. If you keep calm, you will find more strength to be able to tackle everything that anxiety will throw at you.

What Are Your Superpowers?

There have been recent studies that have discovered some amazing superpowers.

What Superpowers Do I Have?

Survival Mode

Three French scientists' (El Zein, Wyart, and Grezes) studies have found that people with anxiety are able to detect threats in just 200 milliseconds.

That's quick! This is far quicker than human beings without anxiety can. A world-class baseball player takes 400 milliseconds to decide what to do when the ball is pitched. We decide threats in HALF THAT TIME! We can be the responsible friend, constantly on the lookout for threats. Willing to take care of everyone.

Increased IQ

Researchers at SUNY DOWNSTATE MEDICAL CENTRE have found that when anxious, we over-analyse our environment, and we need our brains to constantly process information. For our brains to do this, we need a higher IQ! We need more capacity.

Increased Empathic Ability

According to research from psychologists at the department of psychology at the University of Haifa, Israel found that anxious people 'exhibited elevated empathic tendencies'. We can not only have empathic tendencies, but we can also read other people's emotions with a high level of accuracy.

Iron-Will Determination To Keep Going

Every day we cope with anxiety. We keep fighting despite knowing how tough it feels to move forward. We keep going. We do it anyway. Our iron will is required just to appear normal is a colossal superpower!

What Can I Do With These Superpowers?

Higher emotional intelligence helps you be a better leader. It has for me. I see the subtle things that people do, that others miss. I use that to help people to guide them. Even a simple question you ask someone is important.

Use them to drive yourself forward. What we deal with every day we can use to help us break free of anxiety. We have discussed the skills you need in previous chapters.

You can reach out to talk, to be a support and help others and yourself at the same time. That feeling of empowerment you will get by doing a good deed and the feeling you aren't alone will build your self-confidence and greatly enhance your chances of breaking free of anxiety just from this!

What about the future? Could these superpowers actually enhance my life after the worst times of anxiety? Yes, it can.

A higher IQ can be used to gather different information rather than fears, worries, and overthinking. What about reading? Learning? The development of yourself? I am not a doctor, but I have found that I can use my 'higher intelligence' to improve and develop myself more and expand my mind to more possibilities. I have found I am more open to different concepts, and I feel that I see the world very differently to others.

Better emotional intelligence means that you can get on and care about others. This is an awesome skill to have, one that many people would love to have themselves. You can use it to build stronger, deeper friendships and relationships. It will also help you improve your leadership skills. Having high emotional intelligence is one of the most important skills you need in today's business, but few people have it. You will have it in abundance!

What Makes You, YOU?

The daily struggles with anxiety train your mind to deal with the pain. It makes you stronger.

It makes you kinder and more compassionate, caring, and more aware of others. It also makes you more humble. It has made me more driven and determined.

Think for a second what positive effects you have from anxiety?

Why Would You Want To Take Your Anxiety Away?

It would be taking a massive part of me away. It would be like taking my right arm from me. I would be lost.

I have my anxiety by my side. It reminds me every day what is important. My mind-talk doesn't need any excuse to take control aside from being calm and seeing the joy in life. I need my anxiety. I couldn't picture my life without it!

How Do You Leverage Your Anxiety?

Gain control over how you think about what you perceive. Using your anxiety to keep motivated and driven will make your life such a better place.

How I Used My Anxiety Against My Anxiety To Achieve My Goals

This is what I do. I use this method a lot. I don't recommend doing this from the start, as it will only lead you to more anxiety or panic attacks. Once you have more confidence and control through meditation, I have learned to use my fear of failure as an excellent driving force against my anxiety. I focus on what I need to get done for the day and what it would feel like if I completed what I need to get done. Then I focus on what I would feel like if I don't achieve my goals and tell myself it has to be done today or I have failed. I give myself time frames to achieve my goals. I then think of the worst thing that could happen if I don't do it. I get worried, and immediately this sets me to action! That fear of failure is an excellent motivational tool to get you to do what needs to be done.

Once you have completed a goal, reward yourself. I have done a lot of this in the past, and it did push me. I find it exhausting, but I have achieved what I set myself to do. It enhances where I want to go and reminds me that my anxiety and worry are all states of mind. Warning: you have to feel in control of the situation. It isn't intended to give yourself a panic or anxiety attack. The trick is still having control and distance over your anxiety.

I am getting quite adept at using my anxiety to achieve what I need. It breaks through my procrastination and worry. But, it comes with being exhausted and relying on my negative mind talk to keep me going.

How Does Using Your Anxiety Feel?

It is empowering when you have learnt what makes your anxiety come up. You have learnt what strengths you have from anxiety. Using it to your benefit is almost a role reversal. Having that power and control over your anxiety to use it to do what you want is pretty cool. Turning the power against itself is a great strategy. Take in the fear, but do it anyway!

What Does Anxiety Mean To You?

It has control over you. Each day you feel that you are losing the fight. You are losing control of the person you were. Each challenge needs superhuman efforts and it's exhausting. But what if you could turn it against itself and have control over it and could manage and regulate it.

Would you have ever believed that you could love your anxiety? Befriend it? Be able to use it to help you? To move from wanting to be rid of your anxiety because you hate it to being able to love it as part of you?

Congratulations! You have made an important step in your battle!

This Chapter In A Nutshell

- I don't recommend leveraging your anxiety when you are still in a constant battle with anxiety. It will do more harm than good.

- Understand your triggers; understand yourself. Once you understand yourself, you can befriend your anxiety.

- You have four amazing superpowers from anxiety: higher IQ, higher emotional intelligence, an iron will to keep fighting, and the ability to see threats in 200 milliseconds!

- I love my anxiety. I don't want to lose that part of me that gives me direction and an edge in my life.

- I use my fear of failure. More specifically, I use my fear of not achieving to get me motivated and driven. I focus on what would happen if I don't achieve my specific goal. This breaks through my procrastination and worry.

- Love your anxiety. It can be an amazing asset!

Food For Thought

Realisations

Get things wrong, learn, and makes changes as a result of your mistakes.

One of the most important teachings I have had over the last year is that it's important to make mistakes, to get things wrong and fail. Keep failing. We sufferers struggle with the shame and fear of getting things wrong and failing. But life is about experiencing mistakes. The way I learn and develop is by getting things wrong. My resilience is much stronger these days. I bounce back much quicker than I used to. We all struggle in life sometimes. We are all making mistakes, and we are all failing. It's how we respond to them that helps us move forward.

Struggling is important in your aid to be better. Without struggle and pain, how do you grow? How do you appreciate the good things in life without also experiencing the bad?

Understanding that we all struggle is part of rewiring your brain. It's not being as hard on yourself when things do go wrong.

I stop myself when I go over and over and over the conversation in my head. I also want to dissect the call and pull to pieces all the things I said wrong or forgot to mention. Did I come across as calm? Am I giving others a sense of hope with what I am saying?

I have learnt to understand that one of the best gifts I can give is turning up as my authentic, honest self, turning up as me. Not being perfect and showing my vulnerability to others I don't know is a way of being authentic. Not expecting myself to be perfect before I can help others is another way I can show up and serve myself and others. It's really okay to be yourself. People can relate to you.

How do you tackle problems? Approach them not as problems but puzzles.

Look at struggles from a different angle. Life is about learning and growing. It's about putting yourself on the next rung of the ladder.

Realisation Two

Your feelings can't predict the future. When you feel those feelings, they are just feelings at that moment. Watch how your mind then makes judgements and mind-talk from those feelings. I found this a profound learning: your feelings can manipulate your judgements, sometimes extremely irrational judgements.

Realisation Three

We all have bad habits. I don't mean picking your nose. I mean habits that you do over and over again. You may not even realise you do what you do. It's a cycle. By being more present and self-aware, you can see your habits coming back and catch yourself. Recently, I have not done as well as I had hoped. I have also caught myself from pushing myself harder by sacrificing time with my family, giving up sleep, and allowing my anxiety to take over to drive me. I will stay in survival mode. I saw the pattern occurring and stopped myself. I said to myself, *Your best is good enough.* I focused on my breath. I looked back at what I had achieved in the past year. I went over the messages I had received over the last few months, and I told myself that I am making a difference. Look at your progress. Keep following your path. Your adventure will get you to where you want to go but not how you are doing it now.

That leads to not appreciating the journey, not spending time with your family, and becoming a complete burnout.

Food For Thought . . .
When There Is
Nothing Else Left

I have dreams, grand dreams. I demand a lot of myself. I expect too much. I push myself beyond what is reasonable. I do it because I want a different life. I want to do better for my wife and family. I believe that my suffering and life experience can make a difference to others.

Sometimes it not about talent or how good you are.

It's not about how much money you have spent.

It's not about amazing and creative ideas.

Sometimes it's simply about will. It's about your will to keep going when you feel this is a disaster, when you are failing, and when you are struggling to believe in yourself.

When everything you are doing to reach your goals just isn't working and when it feels impossible, so hard to just achieve what you know you need to, you must move forward.

It's about rolling up your sleeves and doing it anyway. It's about showing up.

It's about using that inner strength, that iron will that you used to use just to stay alive in the past, to break down your barriers to keep moving forward when your anxiety is telling you otherwise.

It's about failing, failing, and failing again, but still, keep moving forward. It's learning from those mistakes, reflecting on your performance, and doing better. If you have done wrong and you can fix it, then fix it.

You see, you aren't failing! Your time just isn't here yet.

You can do better. You will get stronger. You will make a difference.

Aim for the stars. I am! You can change the world!

STEP FOUR

Happiness

It's icy cold, the stars are shining brightly.

There isn't a cloud in the sky.

I look up at the sky in wonder.

The hairs stand up on the back of my neck.

The stars look so far away but I can almost grab them.

I see a universe full of amazing possibilities.

I see a path I am loving to walk.

I see how amazing life is, in a moment of joy.

I feel overcome with emotion, tears entering my eyes.

I stand, head up, surveying the stars, and I am awed.

In wonder.

In excitement.

What a life I have.

What a path I am on.

What hope I have!

What a future!

Happiness and Appreciate Everything

'I do believe that if you haven't learned from sadness, you can't appreciate happiness'.
—*Nana Mouskouri*

What Is In This Chapter

Find your happiness within. This chapter is a breakdown of how you can find your happiness. There are several steps to take to achieve it. Happiness is a skill to learn. By the end of this chapter, you will know what to do to unlock and find your happiness.

So much of our lives we are chasing our happiness. We expect that when we get to our goal, we will feel happy. Spoiler alert: we don't. Happiness is not about reaching some destination; it's about appreciating the journey. Now.

Life will throw a lot at you. With all the pain and suffering and moving through challenges, you will truly grow and learn. It's how you tackle what happens that will be the difference.

Life is amazing; it's a game. It has ups and downs. Just when you think that you have life pegged and that it's predictable, something happens to rock your world, whether it is something bad or good.

Your mind decides what your attention, your most important commodity, focuses on. You create your own world. You see life in a completely different way compared to everyone else. Some people will see the same experience completely differently than you.

How to tackle your feelings and how you take on information will decide your perception. Your mind is driven by your emotions. If you feel down or low, you will see and experience the way you feel. It's about rewiring your brain to be more positive. This enhances your resilience.

What Does Your Happiness Feel Like?

Happiness is feeling positive and able to appreciate the good things in life. It's feeling joyful.

Why Have Happiness?

We are all striving to be happy. It's our quest and our holy grail. Having it is a cornerstone to your success in beating anxiety.

Appreciate Everyone

I get frustrated sometimes when loved ones don't see life as I do. I want to shake them. I want them to progress like I have. What I need to appreciate is that everyone is on different journeys and that I shouldn't expect the same from them.

The truth is that only leads to unhappiness, anger, and resentment. I stand back and watch and observe my own feelings and really appreciate what my loved ones do now. The hard work and effort they put in. The love and devotion for what they do. I am thankful for them in my life.

Loved ones are the most important. Taking people on this journey is so important to me. Without them, my progress is meaningless.

I have pushed hard in my life, sometimes at the expense of my loved ones. I know that sacrifices have to be made to realise my dream, but not including my wife and children on the journey isn't a sacrifice I am prepared to take. This drive to be a better me and to achieve my dream of being a successful author and life coach is extremely important. But not at any cost.

The whole reason I am doing this is for my wife and family. I want to show my children that you can do whatever you want to do and show them a better way of life.

Doing Too Much

One of my biggest faults is that, at times, I push myself way too hard! My arrogance of feeling that the rules don't apply to me and I expect more. I feel I have to do everything to not feel I have failed. Not feeling exhausted made me feel I hadn't done enough. Wanting desperately to do all I could was important to me. But what is the cost?

It would exhaust me. It would give away control over my anxiety, allowing it to come back with a vengeance. It would shut off me off from my loved ones. I would make bad decisions and be extremely grumpy and no fun to be around.

I also wouldn't get much done, as I would be too overwhelmed, and I wouldn't be doing as much because I would be too exhausted.

In truth, especially for me, there isn't any real benefit from pushing myself too hard. I have found it more counterproductive, and it slows me up. It's strange when you think that you are doing the exact opposite!

What I have found is, if I push myself too hard, I also struggle to get to sleep, as my mind is frazzled. Even meditation and writing in my journal doesn't help. I have tried several times. After the first set of mediation, nothing helps and it makes me more tired.

Now I plan my time better and bite-size my jobs, removing overwhelm and stress.

My structure I have outlined, but I do plan my week out on a Sunday. Breaking these tasks into bite-size chunks each day, allowing room for manoeuvre, as something always crops up that needs to be done.

I listen to my body and mind. There are times I have to slow down. I need to listen to myself even when jobs haven't been done, and I am not making the big leaps every day in my progress. I have to reframe what I am doing. What's the point if I am jumping forward but the cost is burnout and not appreciating the journey?

Appreciating the journey is important. Spending time with my family and wife has to be part of my growth. I am happy. Doing too much makes this become a chore and removes the joy that I feel each day to be alive, to wake up to the sun coming up. These are the small things that make this life amazing.

I am driven to be the best version of myself and achieve what I have planned at almost any cost. But not at the cost of not having my loved ones with me, liking myself, or appreciating the journey. That's a cost that goes too far.

What Does That Feel Like?

I feel pockets of joy, happy that I appreciate the people around me. I am no longer frustrated or resentful. I feel a weight off my shoulders.

How To Find Your Bliss – Bliss Steps To Success!

Happiness. Being happy. So many people get this wrong. They feel it is a destination. I will feel happy if I win a million pounds or if I find my ideal partner, for example. But the truth is it isn't. Happiness is a skill. It needs to be learned. Happiness is within you. Happiness is right now. It's appreciating what you are, where you are going. Don't get me wrong. This isn't about accepting and being content; they are different feelings altogether. You can still want more from life. I do. But you can still be happy. Appreciate the journey you are on. Take it all in. Allow yourself to enjoy everything that is happening. Enjoy the now. Find your bliss.

Make sure you find time to appreciate the life you have. To say to yourself 'I have done f**king great this week'!

Don't Compare Yourself To Others!

There is an awesome quote that I used in my first book that is relevant here: 'Strive to be a better you'. Try to be better than you were yesterday, and head towards the hero you know you can be. Other people have struggles that you don't know. Comparing yourself to others is a recipe for disaster. Each person terms success differently.

Each person looks at what they don't have.

How Do You Do That?

By rewiring your anxious brain. It's picking up when your mind wanders into negative talk.

When that happens to me, I ask myself if that's a productive use of my time. Take your mind from the emotional side, where your anxiety resides, to your rational side. It will take control back almost immediately. There are other ways to do this. Ask yourself a math question. Even a simple one can move your mind and distract you from the negative mind-talk.

Your feelings are just feelings. In his clarity book, *Less Thinking, More Results*, Jamie Smart describes that your feelings are just making you aware of your thoughts in the moment.

It's like you have different goggles on. Your feelings can't predict the future, and there isn't any sixth sense. Your anxiety is feelings. Don't be fooled into thinking that your feelings can predict the future. One key point to ponder is that your feelings are temporary. They pass.

Reflecting on your week and reviewing what you have done will allow you to see what your progress is. You do this by laying out a structure to your week. I will write down all the jobs I need to get done. I am also realistic. I then split it up and give myself three things to do each day.

Then I tick them off my list. I enjoy putting a big massive tick over the job. I feel a sense of accomplishment!

How Does It Feel Like?

I feel empowered. I am understanding that happiness isn't the destination but the journey itself.

Seeing life in a positive way, I feel that I am enlightened. Strong. Willing to push myself even further from my comfort zone.

Gratitude

We go about our lives, and we don't see what is about us. We don't see the beauty in the world and the important things that make us happy.

By using a journal each night for just five minutes, you can allow yourself the time to appreciate the good things in your day. You can always look back on them.

All I do with mine is split it up into two questions:

What three things I appreciate today?

This could be spending time with my children.

What goal will you achieve tomorrow?

This is getting your mind focused and primed for the next day.

Doing my gratitude journal each night helps to calm me, finish my day on a great note, and set me up for the next day.

Rewiring Your Brain

By consciously challenging your thoughts and meditation, you will able to rewire your brain and remove your negative thoughts. To consciously guide yourself is draining, but you will find, over time, that you will go from having to do it every time, to slowly and naturally thinking differently.

How On Earth Do You Do That?

By asking your mind questions! I usually ask when my mind is worrying about the future, putting up worst-case scenarios in my head because I'm worried about something or generally giving myself a hard time over being me. I ask two simple questions: Is this true? Is this a productive use of my time? I make sure that I come from a point of compassion and love. There is no point in chastising yourself because having a go at yourself defeats the object of the process. This is about loving yourself warts and all. It has to come from a place of kindness. When you do challenge and ask these questions, you move your brain from survival mode, where you are panicking, where you see threats and worry, to the human part of the brain that sees clearly that understands the logical part. Ninety-nine percent of the time the answer is no. Just by asking that question, it should move you away from survival mode because you are switching your brain to think.

What Does It Feel Like?

When I was at my worst, my anxiety would kick in and a particularly bad episode could take me days (if not weeks) to recover. All of this whilst being proactive. Be aware of what your anxiety is saying. Understanding your triggers and challenging your thoughts will lead you to being able to get out of moods more quickly and what you need to do that. Just knowing half the time that you are in an anxiety attack is amazing in itself. But to actually change your mood with your own mind is even better!

With this work, you will be calmer, happier, and have more energy! Not feeling exhausted all the time will also be a benefit.

How Do You Do That?

Start with challenging your thoughts once a day. Get calm. Then, when you are comfortable with that. Increase your challenge to twice, and then three times a day. I would do it when your mind is giving you a hard time.

What would your life be like if you could, from a calm place, see your anxiety hammering you? To know that is happening and be able to use some tools from your swag bag to break it down and quickly?

How would it feel to be able to have more joy in your life? To love yourself? Be compassionate and caring? Be the person you always wanted?

Ponder that.

Slow Down

By using the skills and tools set out in the module you can learn to slow down, take deep breaths during the day, and enjoy what is around you. I love to people-watch. I will watch people in their own worlds, heads down on their phones, coffees in hand. I will look up at the sky and appreciate the sight of a bird soaring over me. I will take deep breaths and just appreciate this moment. I feel a state of calm and contentment, seeing the world for what it is, and understanding the beauty of life.

Learn To Say No

People pleasing isn't a great idea. If you are like me, you want others to be happy, so you put their needs ahead of your own. This leads to you not being able to be your authentic self and drains you. It also aids your anxiety, as it saps your strengths and self-confidence. Learn to say no, learn to understand, and stay true to you.

This Chapter In A Nutshell

- Finding happiness within is a skill that can be learned. It's not a destination. It's the journey itself.

- Feeling happiness is like seeing the positives in any situation, feeling joyful, and being happy with where your life is heading but still striving to do better.

- Appreciating everyone and everything and the loved ones in your life is key to your happiness. Sit back and understand them. See life through their eyes. View them through love, and see how your relationships change. Slow down, even for five minutes a day, and appreciate the life and loves around you.

- Be grateful. Write in a gratitude journal every evening. Just write down three things that you appreciated from your day. Then write down one big goal that you will accomplish tomorrow.

- Challenge your thoughts. Once you have moved into a calm state regularly, you can observe your thoughts a lot more dispassionately and logically. When your mind is hammering you, ask yourself, is this true? Is this a productive use of my time?

- Learn to say no. Stay true to your authentic self. Keep to what you feel is right.

The Beginning Of A New Exciting Journey Having Taken Control Of Your Anxiety

Love your life. Love you. Shine your light.

You have reached the end. Well done. You rock!

You now have a clear direction of what you can do to break your anxiety habit using the four steps.

Thank you for taking the time to read my book. It will help you become the person I know you can be. Dare to dream. What you can be and what you can achieve comes down to you.

Life now is amazing. The internet has been a game changer. You can be a successful, self-published author, YouTube star, or whoever you want to be!

The limit to what you can do is up to you. Perseverance is key. Reflect and move on. Don't let anyone tell you that you can't do it. I have had that regularly.

Your past doesn't matter. What matters is your determination and drive. It takes perseverance and a lot of guts, something we sufferers have in spades!

I have given you plenty of experiences during my recent life. I have shared my struggles and pain to show you that life moves on. You will face struggles, but you will grow from it.

You have seen how much more positive and confident I have become. This could be you!

You have become calmer. You have great hope for the future. You feel happy. How cool is that? Your next chapter in the development of you.

I would love to hear from you. Tell me how this book has helped you. It would be great to hear your stories.

Life has a habit of giving you a curveball. It's how you approach the situation that will set you up.

My life this year has been one of my best. Despite the personal struggles.

FREEDOM OVER ANXIETY

This year I have:

Been promoted twice at work.

Launched a book successfully.

Become an international best selling author. Me! An author selling books!

Achieved the status of bestseller in three countries.

Worked with a life coach.

Become a life coach with clients.

Had my facebook lives viewed by thousands of people.

Helped 100's of anxiety sufferers.

Been a guest speaker on podcasts.

Been on a radio show!

Been a guest speaker at an anxiety and support group.

Met some amazing people.

Made some massive mistakes.

Failed and failed again.

Learned and got better!

What has not been so great:

I have lost a good friend.

My uncle passed away.

Both our cars broke and needed to be replaced!

Could have lost my dad.

You have taken your life to the next level: loving your anxiety, using it to help you achieve your goals. Where do you want to take your life now? Think about that for a second. What can your life be like? Where can you take your life now? I am excited for you. I know what little old me can do, and I know that you can take it further. Also, here's an invitation:

If you want to learn more and want to develop yourself further, then you are more than welcome to message me at mosschristopher799@gmail.com.

Your life will be braver and scarier, in some respects, but exciting; it is in your hands to do whatever you want. Dare to dream. Dare you follow what I have started?

That challenge is up to you. No more feeling like a failure; no more feeling useless and that no one cares. You will be calmer, have more joy, more spirit, and more life!

Following this path and using my four steps will take you away from your struggles. If you follow my advice, you will see what more life has to offer on your terms. Soon you will be feeling the happiest and most driven you have ever felt. You will also know there is oh so much more to come in your life. Exciting times indeed!

One final question to answer:

Now that you have followed my four steps and stuck to the habits outlined in this book, you have likely broken your anxiety habit. Where do you want to take your life now?

I shall leave that for you to answer.

Want the first 6 chapters of my first book *Hope over Anxiety* free?

Please visit:

https://mailchi.mp/b7273d91423c/landingpage

Did You Enjoy Freedom over Anxiety?

If you enjoyed this book, I would greatly appreciate it if you could leave me a review on Amazon.

I know your time is precious, but it will help me improve this book and my future adventures. It will only take a few minutes to do a sentence or two.

Your feedback will be warmly received!

Thank you,

Christopher Moss

Recommended Anxiety Apps

Idonethis – technically not an anxiety app. However it's awesome for writing your day down. Showing how you are feeling. The app reminds you via email and will also give you how you were feeling in the past.

There is a small fee involved.

Calm – this app gets better and better. You have the choice of listening to beautiful calming music, stories or meditation. You can use the free parts. But I would recommend paying the small monthly fee to get the best out of it.

Headspace – I have found some excellent packs focusing on appreciation, anxiety and self-confidence to name a few. Using the body scan, visualisation with some excellent tips on how to get the best from your mediations. There is a free part but I would recommend using the yearly subscription if you can afford it.

Bibliography

Not many books were used in this book. I learned so much from my Life coach Chris Nailor. Many of tools I have learned from him. Mixed in with a few I know.

JAMIE SMART – CLARITY: LESS THINKING MORE RESULTS

DEEPAK CHOPRA – QUANTUM HEALING

BUSTLE.COM – TOOLS TO HELP YOU

Inspiring youtube videos to watch

THE STORY OF YOUR LIFE – DARE TO DO

YOU CAN BE A HERO TOO

DEPRESSION MOTIVATION – BROKEN HEART, ANXIETY AND HARD TIMES

Acknowledgments

I would like to thank my VA and good friend Deanna Baxter for her hard work and advice. Her efforts have pushed this book on even higher. I must have bored her to tears talking to her about this book. Thankfully she has been very gracious.

Otakara Kletke – my accountability partner. She has been awesome in encouraging me to push myself out of my comfort zone and always about to give me advice despite the challenge of time difference.

Jill Rodgers and Kelly Walk Hines thank you for your positive support and help. You have been amazing!

Have you read my first book? Hope over Anxiety?

UK site – www.amazon.co.uk/Hope-over-Anxiety-crippling-anxiety-ebook/dp/B07762F51J/

US site – www.amazon.com/Hope-over-Anxiety-crippling-anxiety-ebook/dp/B07762F51J/

Two New Books of Mine on Anxiety Coming Very Soon

WORKING TITLES – Highly likely these names will change.

Anxiety Bio-hacked – Improving your anxiety through your mind, body and diet. Due Mid-December.

Anxiety and self-confidence – Simple steps to help you feel happier and more confident. Due late December.

52743545R00096

Made in the USA
Columbia, SC
06 March 2019